Out on safari, I saw something neat
A little baby cheetah, light on their feet
Their spots were still fresh, so soft and new
And their fur was so fluffy, it made me coo

But there was something strange, about this little tyke
A silvery stripe of fur, that caught my eye like a spike
I wondered what it was for, this little line so fine
And then I remembered, it's part of their design

The strip helps them hide, from predators up high
Like birds of prey, who might swoop down from the sky
With the silver sheen, the baby cheetah blends in
A tiny trick of nature, so they can avoid a deadly win

As I watched the cub play, I couldn't help but grin
Their energy and spirit, were a delight to take in
And though they were small, they were already so fast
A future champion, born to outlast

Their tiny paws, were soft as can be
And their purring sounds, filled the air with glee
I sat there watching, for what seemed like hours
Enchanted by the sight, of nature's sweet powers

And as the sun set, the baby cheetah ran away
Back to their family, where they'll stay
But I'll never forget, the joy that I found
In that little cheetah, with their silver strip so profound

For it's a reminder, of how nature's so grand
And how every little creature, has a trick up its hand
So let's cherish each moment, with wonder and awe
And celebrate the beauty, of nature in all its raw.

Out on safari, with my jeep in tow,
I spotted a lioness, on the go.
She had a cub, so small and sweet,
And she carried him, with nimble feet.

Through the grasslands, they'd roam and roam,
The lioness and her cub, finding a home.
She'd carry him here, and carry him there,
Looking for a place, with utmost care.

I watched them closely, day after day,
As they wandered along, in their own way.
And every time, the lioness would stop,
And pick up her cub, to reach the top.

She'd carry him high, on her strong back,
Through the savannah, no time to slack.
And as they went, I began to see,
The love between them, so clear to me.

For in the wild, there are dangers untold,
And a mother's love, is worth its weight in gold.
So the lioness carried her cub, every day,
To keep him safe, in every way.

And though I never saw them again,
The memory of that sight, will forever remain.
A mother's love, in the wild so rare,
Carrying her cub, with such tender care.

Ten days old, a baby leopard,
Eyes open wide, all bright and eager.
Crawling around, exploring new sights,
Discovering the world with all its might.

Its spots so dark and fur so soft,
This little leopard is sure aloft.
Dreaming of hunting and running free,
One day a strong and mighty leopard it will be.

But for now, it relies on its mother's care,
Her warmth and love, always there.
Playing with siblings, learning to pounce,
Growing up strong with every ounce.

As the days go by, it starts to grow,
Its curiosity and courage begin to show.
Exploring further, it ventures out,
With a sense of adventure, there's no doubt.

The world is vast and filled with wonder,
From the smallest ants to the biggest thunder.
The baby leopard sees it all,
With eyes wide open, standing tall.

In the distance, it spots a prey,
With a hunter's instinct, it starts to play.
Creeping closer, it pounces with grace,
And in a flash, it has won the race.

Oh, baby leopard, with eyes so bright,
May your spirit forever take flight.
Run wild and free, and never lose sight,
Of the beauty in this world, day or night.

For you are a symbol of strength and power,
A reminder of life's sweetest hour.
Growing strong with each passing day,
And ready to conquer the world, come what may.

Once upon a time, in Africa's vast plains,
A baby rhino was feeling some pains,
For all of her friends, with their horns held high,
Made her feel small, like she couldn't quite fly.

"Wait just a minute," the baby rhino said,
"I know I'll grow a horn atop my head,
Then I'll be strong, and I'll be tall,
And I won't feel small, not at all."

So she waited and waited, day after day,
Hoping her horn would grow, in its own way,
She tried to hurry it up, with all her might,
But her horn wouldn't budge, try as she might.

She looked to her friends, and let out a sigh,
For they were still bigger, and she wondered why,
"Why won't my horn grow?" she asked with a frown,
"I want to be like you, the biggest around."

Her friends just smiled, and said with a grin,
"Your horn will grow, don't worry, don't spin,
Just be patient, and in time you'll see,
Your horn will grow, just wait and let it be."

So the baby rhino sat and waited some more,
Hoping her horn would finally soar,
And as she sat and waited, day after day,
Her horn finally grew, in its own way.

And now she's strong, and she's tall,
And she doesn't feel small, not at all,
For her horn may be small, but it's just the right size,
And it makes her feel big, like she can touch the skies.

A baby elephant, just born today,
Was eager to learn and to play.
But there was one thing he couldn't quite do,
And that was to use his trunk, it was all so new.

His trunk was long and floppy and gray,
He tried to pick things up, but it wouldn't obey.
He watched his mom and dad with great care,
And wondered when he would learn to be fair.

One day, he saw his mom pick up a leaf,
With her trunk so dexterous, it was beyond belief.
He tried and tried, but he couldn't quite grasp,
The leaf kept slipping, he let out a gasp.

But then he saw a butterfly flitting by,
And he knew he had to give it a try.
He reached out with his trunk and gave a blow,
And to his surprise, the butterfly did go.

He laughed and trumpeted with such glee,
He knew he was on his way to being free.
Free to explore and to play with his trunk,
He was no longer feeling like such a funk.

So now the baby elephant can use his trunk with ease,
And he can pick up leaves, fruit, and even the breeze.
He's happy and content with all that he's learned,
And he can't wait to see what else he's earned.

Once upon the savannah, in the middle of the day,
A baby wildebeest was born, cute and curious in every way.
His legs were wobbly, his nose was wet,
And he looked around with wonder, not knowing what to expect.

His mother licked him clean, and then she nuzzled him close,
And the baby wildebeest felt loved, more than anyone knows.
But as the sun rose high, the herd began to move,
And the baby wildebeest had to learn to run, if he wanted to groove.

At first he stumbled, and his legs tangled up,
He fell on his nose, and he spilled his milk cup.
But his mother was patient, and his siblings were kind,
And they helped him up, so he wouldn't be left behind.

With every step he took, the baby wildebeest grew stronger,
He learned to leap and bound, and to run even longer.
And before he knew it, he was running with the herd,
Proud and free, like a mighty wildebeest bird.

Now he runs with the others, through the grass and the dust,
His heart beating fast, his muscles fit for the thrust.
And when the sun sets low, and the herd settles down,
The baby wildebeest knows he's grown, and he wears his new crown.

For he's learned to run with the best, to keep up with the pace,
And he's ready for whatever challenges come his way in this place.
So if you ever see a baby wildebeest, stumbling and unsure,
Just remember, with a little help, he can become a champion for sure!

On the African plain, a time ago,
A baby antelope felt such woe.
The grass was dry and hard to chew,
The little one didn't know what to do.

Then the skies opened up one day,
Rain poured down in a lovely way.
The baby antelope felt so free,
It pranced and skipped with joyful glee.

Following the rain, it searched for grass,
Supple, tender, easy to amass.
It hopped and skipped, hardly took rest,
Till it found what it deemed the best.

The grass it found was soft and low,
It ate and ate till it ceased to grow.
With tummy full, it lay to rest,
Feeling cool, its thirst now blessed.

Whenever rain comes down these days,
The baby antelope wears no dismays.
For it knows that the rain will bring
Sweet, tender grass for its fling.

A baby ostrich, oh so small,
Tried to run but would always fall.
Its long legs were quite a sight,
But balancing them just wasn't right.

One day it tried to spread its wings,
To see if they could do some things.
It flapped them hard and off it went,
Running with a newfound strength.

The baby ostrich stumbled at first,
Its wings flapping, almost burst.
But with each step it grew more sure,
Its wings now helping it to endure.

It ran and ran, all around,
Its wings keeping it off the ground.
And though it stumbled here and there,
It never gave up, it didn't despair.

For the baby ostrich knew one day,
It would run and fly, in its own way.
And so it practiced every day,
Until it could balance in every way.

And now the baby ostrich is grown,
Its wings and legs fully honed.
It runs and flies with such grace,
A true wonder of the ostrich race.

In the tall grass, oh what a sight,
A baby zebra, so black and white,
But wait, what's this? It's hard to see,
The stripes on this zebra blend perfectly!

With stripes so bold, and stripes so fine,
This baby zebra knows how to shine,
In the grass so green, it's hard to tell,
Where the zebra ends, and the grasses dwell.

Its stripes help it hide, like camouflage,
From predators that might cause it harm,
And so the baby zebra can play and roam,
In the grasses tall, it has found a home.

But the zebra wasn't always this way,
When it was born, it was quite a display,
With stripes so bright, they shone like the sun,
The baby zebra's disguise wasn't yet done.

So it learned to blend in, and match its surround,
Using its stripes, it stayed safe and sound,
And now it's a master, a pro at the game,
A baby zebra hiding in plain sight, what a name!

So if you see a zebra, black and white,
Look closely, you might be in for a surprise,
For this baby zebra has a clever disguise,
With stripes that make it blend, oh so wise!

And as it grows up, it'll continue to change,
Its stripes will shift, and its patterns rearrange,
But one thing stays constant, in every stage,
The zebra's stripes will always help it engage.

So let's learn from the zebra, and its clever ways,
And blend in with our world, in similar displays,
We might not have stripes, but we have other traits,
That can help us hide, and avoid any fate.

A baby Giraffe so tall and lean,
Just moments old, with spots unseen,
He wobbles and sways, with legs so spindly,
But soon he'll stand up, oh so kindly.

His mama nudges him, with her long neck,
And whispers to him, "Don't you fret,
You'll soon be up, standing so tall,
And we'll run and play, all in all."

With each try, he gets a bit closer,
His legs unsteady, but growing bolder,
Until one moment, he finds his feet,
And stands up straight, oh so neat!

The other animals gather 'round,
To see the little Giraffe they've found,
And they cheer and clap, as he stands so proud,
For he's learned to stand, amidst the crowd.

So now he walks, with grace and ease,
With each step, he feels the breeze,
And he knows, with each passing day,
He'll grow up strong, in every way.

He stretches his neck up high,
Reaching for leaves in the sky,
His spots are bright, his eyes are wide,
As he explores the world outside.

He runs and jumps, with youthful glee,
His mother watches, patiently,
And though he still has much to learn,
He's growing up, at every turn.

As he matures, he'll tower above,
The animals he used to love,
And though he'll miss being small,
He'll be the tallest of them all.

But for now, he's just a little guy,
With a gleam in his eye,
Ready to take on the world,
With a confidence, yet to unfurl.

Deep down in the river's flow,
Where bubbles danced and currents slowed,
There lived a little hippo child,
So sweet and plump and oh so mild.

With chubby cheeks and shining eyes,
He'd wiggle, giggle, and surprise,
The other hippos with his tricks,
As he bounced across the rocks, no need for kicks.

He'd twist and turn, then jump so high,
And land with a satisfying sigh.
The fish would swirl around his path,
And bubbles would tickle him as he passed.

The other hippos stood in awe,
As the baby hippo stole the floor.
With every bounce and every skip,
His little hooves would barely dip.

The river's secrets were his to keep,
As he'd explore and then would leap,
To new adventures, hidden streams,
And underwater worlds, like in his dreams.

And when the night would come to call,
The little hippo'd have a ball,
But then he'd know it's time to go,
And bounce across the rocks, back to his home.

And so the little hippo child,
Kept bouncing with a heart so wild,
Through every ripple, every tide,
Across the rocks, he'd gracefully glide.

A baby baboon, so small and round,
In the African savannah, it was found,
Protected from weather, safe and sound,
By mother and father, who stand so tall and bound.

When the clouds grow dark and the rain starts pouring,
The baboon family finds a spot, not ignoring,
And huddles together until it fades,
Keeping baby baboon out of the rain blades.

When the wind starts blowing with all its might,
Mother and father hold on tight,
And keep baby baboon out of sight,
Until the wind passes in the night.

When the sun is blazing, they find a tree,
And bask in the shade, just them three,
They groom each other, with love and care,
And baby baboon feels their warmth and air.

Through all the elements, they stand strong,
Protecting baby baboon all day long,
And in the end, when the day is done,
Baby baboon sleeps, feeling loved and warm.

As the stars twinkle and the night grows deep,
Mother and father baboon stay wide awake,
Keeping a watchful eye on baby baboon's sleep,
So predators won't come and cause an earthquake.

In the morning, as the sun rises high,
The baboon family sets out with a sigh,
Searching for food, playing, and running wild,
Making sure baby baboon is never defiled.

Days turn to weeks, weeks turn to months,
The baboon family continues to grow and have fun,
And baby baboon learns from mother and father,
How to be strong, resilient, and gather.

And as the years pass by,
Baby baboon turns to an adult, with a sigh,
But the lessons and love from mother and father,
Will remain with baby baboon forever after.

There was a baby crocodile,
A tiny creature with a smile,
And as he swam along the Nile,
He loved to play and splash awhile.

But crocs and other beasts of prey,
Would lurk around and spoil his day,
So he'd retreat to mom, and stay,
Safe in her mouth as she'd make way.

His mother's mouth was wide and strong,
A place where baby felt belong,
With teeth so sharp and eyes so keen,
She kept her baby snug and clean.

Through the reeds and through the mud,
The baby croc had nothing to dread,
For in his mother's mouth he'd ride,
With her he'd always be by his side.

And though it may seem strange to us,
For baby croc, it was a plus,
To be inside that cavernous,
Jawline, that was so advantageous.

He'd watch the world pass by him fast,
And wonder what it was at last,
But then he'd smile and rest at last,
Knowing that mom would guide him past.

So if you see them pass you by,
Don't you worry, don't you cry,
For baby croc is safe and sound,
With mother's love, he'll be well found.

And when he's grown and big and strong,
He'll know that he can't do no wrong,
For in his heart, he'll feel the throng,
Of a mother's love, that's so lifelong.

Once upon a time, in a nest up high,
A baby vulture was born, with a bald spot, oh my!
His feathers were scruffy, his beak sharp and long,
But atop his head, there was nothing but skin, all along.

The other birds in the forest saw him and scoffed,
"Look at his head, it's totally aloft!"
But the baby vulture didn't mind their jeer,
He waddled around with his parents, with no fear.

They flew high and swooped low, but the baby couldn't fly,
He was too small, so he watched and wondered why.
But he never lost hope, he knew he'd grow up,
And when he did, he'd soar high, not just look up.

As he grew older, his feathers began to sprout,
And the bald spot was no more, he could stand tall and shout.
He flapped his wings, and took off in the sky,
And all the other birds watched, as he flew by.

The baby vulture had become a strong bird,
And in the forest, he was now well-liked and heard.
He soared through the clouds with such grace,
And looked down on the forest with a peaceful face.

But he never forgot where he came from,
And the teasing that once made him feel so dumb.
For he knew that being different was just fine,
And that what really mattered was what's inside, divine.

So if you ever see a vulture with a bald spot on his head,
Remember the baby vulture and what he said.
That even if you don't look like the rest,
You can still be the best, and soar with the best.